The Christ of Cynewulf: A Poem in Three Parts: The Advent, the Ascension, and the Last Judgment

Cynewulf

THE
CHRIST OF CYNEWULF

A Poem in Three Parts

THE ADVENT, THE ASCENSION, AND
THE LAST JUDGMENT

TRANSLATED INTO ENGLISH PROSE

BY

CHARLES HUNTINGTON WHITMAN
FELLOW IN ENGLISH OF YALE UNIVERSITY

———•———

BOSTON, U.S.A.
GINN & COMPANY, PUBLISHERS
The Athenæum Press
1900

PREFACE.

My purpose in the present translation is so to combine
faithfulness with literary quality as to afford reasonable
satisfaction to both the specialist and the general student
of literature. In my diction I have endeavored to avoid
unintelligible archaisms, and have sought after simple
idioms, with a preference for words of Germanic origin.

masculine!!

All things considered, prose has been adopted as the
most satisfactory medium of translation. Verse may be
the ideal form, but it requires an ideal translator; and with
the exception of Tennyson's version of *The Battle of Bru-
nanburh*, and perhaps one or two others, I can think of
none that are at all adequate. Nor is prose without its
peculiar advantages; in at least one important respect it
is superior to verse, since its flexibility offers a more facile
medium for reproducing that metrical variety which is one
of the principal charms of Old English poetry.

Up to the present time there have appeared three
complete translations of this poem — Thorpe's in his
edition of the *Codex Exoniensis*, Gollancz's in his two
editions of the *Christ*, and Grein's in his *Dichtungen der
Angelsachsen*. I have made free use of these translations,
and am indebted to them for an occasional word or phrase.

The line-numbering follows the original, which neces-
sarily causes irregular intervals between the marginal
numbers. Square brackets indicate words inserted by
the translator for the sake of clearness.

This translation was undertaken at the suggestion of Professor Albert S. Cook, and closely conforms in readings and punctuation to his recent edition of the *Christ*. Through his kindness I have been furnished with the proof-sheets as needed, and have thereby found my labor materially lessened. Specific acknowledgments to this edition are usually made in the foot-notes, but many of the Biblical parallels come from the same source. Throughout my work I have had the benefit of Professor Cook's ripe scholarship and sound judgment; for his unfailing kindness and helpfulness I wish to express my deep sense of gratitude. It also gives me pleasure to acknowledge my indebtedness to Mr. Robert K. Root, who has carefully read the whole of my manuscript; and to Dr. Charles G. Osgood and Dr. Frank H. Chase for various helpful suggestions.

The introduction to Professor Cook's volume relieves me from attempting a literary appreciation. Suffice it to say that, as the beauties of the *Christ* have gradually unfolded before me, I have come to feel that it is the most spiritual expression of an age in which poetry, vital and genuine, if somewhat unformed, welled directly from the deeps of man's nature.

If this translation should serve to win even a few readers to an ardent and appreciative love of Old English verse, the author would feel amply rewarded; yet the fitting and adequate recompense of such labor as it has cost lies in the disclosure to the soul of the worker of a beauty and truth hitherto unapprehended.

Yale University,
April 12, 1900.

THE CHRIST.

—•◦•—

PART I.—THE ADVENT.

———to the King.

Thou art the corner-stone which the builders once rejected in their work ; fitting indeed is it for Thee, O King of glory, to become the head of this noble temple, and to join in bond secure the broad walls of adamantine rock, so that throughout the cities of earth all things endowed with sight may wonder[1] evermore. Reveal then, righteous and triumphant One, through Thy wisdom, Thine own handiwork, and leave wall firm against wall. The work hath need that the Master Builder, the King Himself, should come and forthwith restore the house that beneath its roof hath fallen into ruin. He formed the body, the limbs of clay ; and now is it time for Him, the Prince of life, to deliver this miserable host from their enemies, the wretched from their fears, as He full oft hath done.

[1] The construction in lines 7 and 8 is largely conjectural. Cf. Cook's *Christ*, p. 74.

O Ruler and righteous King, Thou who holdest
20 the key and openest life, bless us with victory, with
that glorious success denied unto him whose work
availeth naught ! Verily in our need do we speak
these words : We beseech[1] Him who created man
that He choose not to pronounce judgment upon us
25 who, sad at heart, sit yearning in prison for the
sun's joyous course until such time as the Prince of
life reveal light unto us, become our soul's defense,
and compass the feeble mind with splendor ; of all
30 this may He make us worthy, we whom He admitted
to glory, when, deprived of our heritage, we were
doomed to turn in wretchedness unto this narrow
land. Therefore he who speaks truth may say that
when the race of men was turned away [from God],
35 He saved it. Young was the virgin, a sinless
maiden, whom He chose for His mother ; it was
brought to pass without the embraces of man that
the bride became great with child.[2] Never before
40 or after in this world was there conception of woman
like unto that ; it was secret, a mystery of the Lord.
All spiritual grace overspread the regions of earth ;
then was many a wise saying illumined by the Lord
of life, such ancient teaching, prophetic song, as of old

---

[1] Manuscript defective at lines 23 and 24. Cf. Cook's *Christ*, p. 77.
[2] The phrase *ðurh bearnes gebyrd* omitted in translation.

lay wrapped in darkness, when the Ruler came who 45
magnifieth the course [1] of their words who wisely desire to praise without stint the name of the Creator.

O vision of peace, holy Jerusalem, best of royal 50
thrones, city of Christ, native abode of angels, in
thee alone the souls of the righteous rest ever,
rejoicing in their glory! Never shall trace of sin
be brought to light in that dwelling-place, but all 55
iniquity, all curse and strife, shall flee far from thee.
Thou art gloriously full of holy joy, as thy name
bears witness. Behold now thyself how the wide
creation round about and the vault of heaven regard 60
thee far and near on every side; [2] the King of
heaven seeketh thee in His course, yea, cometh Himself and taketh up His abode in thee, as long ago
wise prophets spake in words, when they proclaimed
the birth of Christ, told it for thy joy, thou chiefest 65
of cities. Now is the Child come, born to interpret
and fulfill [3] the works of the Jews. He bringeth
thee joy; He looseneth thy bonds; He draweth
nigh [4] to men, for He knoweth their wants — how
the wretched must needs await succor. 70

[1] With evident reference to 2 Thess. 3. 1.

[2] This interpretation does not conform to the Antiphon. Cf. Cook's *Christ*, p. 83.

[3] *Tō wyrpe*, the noun suggesting the pregnant sense of 'transform.'   [4] Reading *genēhwað* with Cook.

O thou joy of women in heavenly glory, fairest of
all maidens throughout the regions of earth, so far
as ocean-dwellers have ever learned, reveal to us
the mystery that came to thee from the skies,
75 how thou didst ever conceive so that a child might
be born, and yet hadst[1] not at all carnal intercourse
after the manner of men! Of a truth we have never
heard that in days of old there came to pass such a
80 thing as thou didst receive by special grace, nor may
we look for such an event in time to come. Truly a
noble faith dwelt in thee, for thou didst bear within
thy womb the Lord of glory, and yet thy splendid
85 virginity was not defiled. All the children of men, as
they sow in tears, even thus they reap — they bring.
forth unto death. Then spake the blessed maiden,
the holy Mary, ever full of triumph: 'Why marvel
90 ye thus, why grieve ye and sorrowfully lament, ye
sons and daughters of Salem? Ye ask in curiosity
how I preserved my virginity, my chastity, and yet
became the mother of God's illustrious Son? Verily
95 the secret is not known unto men, but Christ declared
that in David's beloved daughter all the guilt of Eve
is blotted out, the curse removed, and the weaker
100 sex exalted. Hope hath arisen that a blessing amid
the joy of heavenly angels, with the Father of right-

---

[1] Lit. 'knewest.'

·eousness, may now abide for both men and women evermore through all eternity.'

Lo ! Thou Splendor of the dayspring, fairest of angels sent to men upon earth, Thou Radiance of 105 the Sun of righteousness, bright beyond the stars, Thou of Thy very self dost illumine all the tides of time ! Even as Thou, God begotten of God, Son of the true Father, didst ever dwell without begin- 110 ning in the glory of heaven, so Thine own handi- work in its present need imploreth Thee with con- fidence that Thou send us the bright sun, and come in Thy very person to enlighten those who have long 115 been covered with murky cloud, and sitting here in darkness and eternal night, shrouded in sins, have been forced to endure the shadow of death. Now in the fulness of hope we believe in the salvation brought to men through the Word of God, who was in the be- 120 ginning co-eternal with God the Father almighty, and afterward became flesh without blemish, being born ⌒ of the virgin as a help for the afflicted. God appeared among us without sin ; the mighty Son of God and 125 the Son of Man dwelt together in harmony among mankind. Wherefore it is right that we should ever give thanks by our deeds[1] unto the Lord of

[1] The rendering of *bi gewyrhtum* is here somewhat doubtful.

victory, for that He was willing to send Himself unto us.

130   O God of spirits, how wisely and how rightly wast Thou named Emmanuel, as the angel first called it in Hebrew, which, fully interpreted in its hidden meaning, is : 'Now is God Himself with us, the
135 Guardian of the skies!' Even so of yore ancient men foretold the coming of the King of kings, the spotless Priest. Thus long ago the great Melchisedec, wise of spirit, revealed the divine majesty of
140 the eternal Ruler. He was the bringer of laws and precepts to those who had long looked. for His advent; for it was promised them that by the power of the Spirit the Son of the Creator would Him-
145 self pass through the regions of earth, and visit the lowest depths. Now were they waiting patiently in captivity until the Son of God should come unto them in their sorrow. And thus they spake, prostrated
150 by suffering: 'Come now Thyself, high King of heaven. Bring salvation unto us wretched prisoners, worn out with weeping, with bitter burning tears. In Thee alone is relief for those in dire need. Seek[1]
155 us here, captives sad of heart ; leave not[2] behind Thee, when Thou goest hence, a multitude so great ;

1 Reading *gesēce* with Gollancz.   2 Reading *ne lǣt* with Gollancz.

but do Thou royally manifest Thy compassion upon us, O Christ our Savior, Prince of glory ; let not the accursed have dominion over us.   Leave unto us the eternal joy of Thy glory, that those whom Thou didst 160 first create with Thine hands may worship Thee, the radiant King of hosts, who dwellest eternally on high with God the Father.'

[*Mary*]. 'Alas my Joseph, son of Jacob, descendant of the great king David, art thou bound to break 165 off thy firm troth and forsake my love ? '

[*Joseph*]. ' I am full deeply troubled, bereft of my good name ; on thy account I have heard many words, boundless causes of grief,[1] taunts and con- 170 tumely ; they utter insults and many reproaches against me.   Sad in spirit I must needs pour out my tears.   God alone[2] can easily heal the sorrow of my heart and comfort me in my misery.   Alas young damsel, maiden Mary ! '   175

[*Mary*]. 'Why grievest thou and criest out in sorrow ?   Never have I found in thee any fault, or cause for suspicion that thou hast wrought evil ; and yet thou speakest these words as if thou thyself wert filled with every sin and iniquity.'   180

[1] Lit. ' griefs.'
[2] So the sense seems to require, though the word is lacking in the text.

[*Joseph*]. ‘ I have endured too much misery because of this child-bearing. How can I refute their hateful words, or find any answer to my enemies ? •It is known
185 far and wide that from the glorious temple of the Lord I willingly received a pure maiden free from sin, and now all is changed by I know not what. Neither speech nor silence avails me aught. If I declare the
190 truth, then must the daughter of David perish, slain with stones. Yet is it harder for me to conceal crime ; as a perjurer I should be forced to live thenceforth, hated of all peoples, despised among the tribes of men.’
195 Then the maid unraveled the mystery, and thus she spake : ‘ I swear truly by the Son of God, the Savior of souls, that I have never yet had intercourse with
200 any man on earth ; but it was granted unto me, while yet young in my home, that Gabriel, heaven’s archangel, bade me hail, and said in truth that the heavenly Spirit would shine upon me with His splendor, and that I should bear the Glory of life, an
205 illustrious Child, the great Son of God, the bright King of glory. Now without guilt have I been made His temple ; the Spirit of comfort hath dwelt within me. Do thou henceforth forego all grievous care. Give eternal thanks unto God’s great Son
210 that I have become His mother, though still a maiden, and that thou art reputed His earthly father

in the thoughts of men; thus was prophecy to be truly fulfilled in Himself.'

O Thou King of kings, righteous and peaceful, Christ almighty, how didst Thou spring into being 215 with Thy glorious Father before all the hosts of the world, a child begotten by His power and might! There is now no man under heaven, no hero so exceeding wise and prudent that he can relate or 220 truly explain to the ocean-dwellers how the Guardian of the skies took Thee in the beginning for His noble Son. Of all the things created under the welkin, so far as the race of men[1] hath heard among the peoples, first did the wise God, Author of life, 225 divide in majesty the light from the darkness. His was the power of decision, and the Lord of hosts gave this command : 'Let there be a bright light henceforth for ever and ever, a joy to all living men 230 who in their generations shall be born.'

And straightway it came to pass when it was so to be ; a light, bright amidst the stars, shone forth for the nations of men after the lapse of time ; Himself 235 ordained that Thou, His Son, shouldst be co-dwelling with Thine only Lord before aught of this should ever come to pass. Thou art that Wisdom who

---

[1] Lit. 'nations.'

240 with the Lord didst frame all this broad creation. Wherefore there is no one so wise and prudent that he can clearly set forth Thy parentage unto the sons of men. Come now, O Prince of victory, Lord of 245 mankind, and graciously show Thy favor here ; we all desire to understand the mystery of Thy maternal descent, since we can no further unfold Thy 250 paternal lineage. O Savior Christ, by Thine advent graciously bless this world, and the golden gate,[1] which full long stood locked in ages past, do Thou, high Lord of heaven, give command to open ; do Thou visit us, coming in Thy very person humbly to 255 earth. We have need of Thy help. The accursed wolf,[2] that dark shadow of death, hath scattered Thy flock, O Lord, driven it far and wide ; those whom[3] Thou, O sovereign Prince, didst redeem with Thy 260 blood, those[4] the evil one cruelly oppresseth and taketh captive against our will.[5] Wherefore, O Savior, we earnestly pray Thee in the thoughts of our hearts that straightway Thou grant help unto us unhappy exiles ; that the baleful destroyer[6] may

---

[1] Lit. 'gates,' and so 321.

[2] Professor Cook calls attention to Bugge's theory that the Fenris wolf of Old Norse poetry is an imaginative reflex of the Christian conception. Cf. *The Home of the Eddic Poems*, Grimm Library, pp. lvii, lxxiii ff.   [3] Lit. 'what.'   [4] Lit. 'that.'

[5] Lit. 'contrary to the longing of our desires.'

[6] Lit. 'slayer of torment'; perhaps = 'slayer dwelling in torment.'

fall headlong into the abyss of hell; and that Thy 265 handiwork, O Creator of men, may arise and come, as is fitting, to that fair heavenly kingdom whence the dark spirit, through our love of sin, erstwhile enticed and beguiled us, so that, stripped of glory, 270 we must evermore endure misery, unless Thou, Lord eternal, living God, Protector of all creatures, wilt speedily free us from the universal foe.

O renowned throughout the world, purest of 275 women upon earth of those who ever were born, how with joyful heart do all men endowed with speech, all heroes throughout the world, rightly declare and say that thou art the bride of heaven's most 280 excellent King! Even so in the skies the highest retainers of Christ proclaim and sing that in thy holy virtues[1] thou art queen of the heavenly host, of the 285 ranks of men under heaven, and of the dwellers in hell; for thou alone of all mankind with splendid courage didst resolve to bring thy virginity unto the Lord, and offer it up without sin. No ring-adorned 290 bride like unto thee hath since come among men, bringing in due time with pure heart that fair offering to the heavenly home. Wherefore the Lord triumphant bade His archangel fly hither from the majesty 295

[1] Or, 'powers.'

of His glory, and straightway reveal to thee the fulness of His power, that thou, Mary, in compassion for
mankind, shouldst bear in pure nativity the Son of
300 God, and shouldst keep thyself unspotted for ever.
We have heard also that long ago in days of old a
righteous prophet, Isaiah,[1] spake concerning thee,
[saying] that he was led where he fully beheld the
305 mansions of life in the eternal abode.   Then the
wise prophet looked out over that region, till he saw
where there was set a noble portal.   The towering
gate was bound all about with precious metal, begirt
310 with wondrous bands.   He fully believed that no
man unto all eternity could ever lift bars so firmly
fixed, or open the fastening of that city-gate, until
315 the angel of God, with benign purpose, made known
the manner of it, and spake these words: 'I can
declare to thee the truth[2] that in course of time God
320 Himself, the Father almighty, will pass by the power
of the Spirit through this golden gate, and through
these firm barriers will visit earth; and after
Him it shall for evermore remain so tightly locked
325 that, save God the Redeemer, none shall ever again
open it.'

Now is that fulfilled which the wise one there

---

[1] Properly, 'Ezekiel.'
[2] Lit. 'that it has truly come to pass.'

looked upon with his very eyes. Thou art that door; through thee the sovereign Lord once issued forth upon this earth, and even thus did Christ almighty find thee adorned with virtues, pure and elect ; so 330 also did the Prince of angels, Giver of life, close thee after Him with a key, [still] free from all blemish. Show now unto us the grace which God's messenger, 335 the angel Gabriel, brought to thee. Lo ! the dwellers in cities beseech thee that thou grant to the peoples this comfort, even thine own Son. Henceforth we may all rejoice with one accord, now that 340 we behold the child [lying] on thy breast. Plead for us now with bold words, that He suffer us no longer to hearken unto error in this valley of death, but that He bring us to the Father's kingdom, where, 345 free from sorrow, we may thenceforth dwell in glory with the Lord of hosts.

O holy Lord of heaven, Thou wast in ages past co-existent with Thy Father in that noble abode ! 350 There was as yet no angel created, nor any of the mighty host who, in the heavens on high, watch over the kingdom, the palace of the Prince, and His service, when Thou, together with God eternal, wast 355 first establishing the wide creation, all these spacious realms. The Holy Ghost, Spirit of comfort, pro-

ceedeth equally from[1] you both. O Christ Jesus,
God the Savior, humbly do we all beseech Thee to
360 hearken unto the voice of these captives, Thy bond-
slaves, how we are tormented by our own desires.
Evil spirits, those hateful hell-fiends, have cruelly
confined us wretched exiles, and bound us with
365 grievous cords. Relief rests in Thee alone, O Lord
eternal. Help Thou the sorrowful, that Thine
advent may comfort the miserable, though we,
through our lust for sin, have waged war upon
370 Thee. Have mercy now upon Thy servants, and
consider our woes — how, feeble in spirit, we stum-
ble here, and wander miserably about. Come now,
O King of men, tarry not too long. We have need
of Thy mercy — that Thou deliver us, O righteous
375 One, and grant us Thy saving grace, that henceforth
we may ever do the better things and work Thy
will among the people.

O Thou glorious heavenly Trinity, full of honor,
380 high and holy, blessed far and wide over the spacious
plains, rightly should those endowed with speech,
wretched dwellers on earth, praise Thee highly with
all their might, now that God, the faithful Savior,
hath revealed unto us that we may know Him!

[1] Lit. 'is common to.'

Wherefore the righteous band of seraphim, with 385
glory crowned, ever chanting fervently with angels
on high, in unwearied hosts sing adoringly with
voices clear and sweet, afar and near. Theirs is 390
the noblest of ministries before the King. Christ
granted them that with their eyes they might enjoy
His presence,[1] and, clothed with ethereal radiance,
ever worship the King far and wide; with their
wings they guard the presence of the Lord almighty 395
and eternal, and press forward toward the throne,
eager who shall hover closest to our Savior within
the courts of peace. They praise the Beloved, and 400
in splendor speak these words to Him, magnifying
the noble Author of all creatures: 'Holy art Thou,
holy, Lord of archangels, righteous King of victory;
O Lord of lords, ever art Thou holy; ever doth Thy 405
glory dwell with men on earth, magnified far and
near throughout all time. Thou art God of hosts,
for Thou, O Shield of warriors, Protector of all
beings, hast filled the heavens and the earth with
the majesty of Thy glory. Hosanna[2] unto Thee in 410
the highest, and on earth praise, renowned among
men. Blessed mayst Thou live, Thou who in the

[1] Cf. Job 19. 26; Ps. 17. 15; Isa. 33. 17; 1 John 3. 2; Rev. 22. 4.
[2] Lit. 'Eternal praise'; used as equivalent to 'Hosanna.' Cf.
Cook's *Biblical Quotations in Old English Prose Writers*, p. 164.

name of the Lord didst come unto the multitudes, a
comfort to the wretched.   To Thee be laud eternal
₄₁₅ ever in the highest, world without end.'

Lo'! how wondrous is the change in the life of
men, that the gentle Creator of mankind took from
a virgin flesh undefiled ; she knew not at all the
embraces of man ; the Lord of triumph came not to
₄₂₀ earth through the seed of man ; but it was a marvel
greater than all the dwellers on earth could understand in its hidden meaning, how the Glory of the
skies, heaven's high Lord, brought help to mankind
₄₂₅ through His mother's womb.   So continually the
Savior of mankind, the Lord of hosts, doth each day
bestow His forgiveness as a help to men.   Wherefore
we, eager for renown, should loyally praise Him both
₄₃₀ in word and deed.   That is surpassing wisdom for
every man who hath an understanding heart, that he
ever worship God most sincerely and earnestly.
₄₃₅ Him shall the hallowed Savior reward for his love
in the country where as yet he hath not come, in the
joy of the land of the living, where he shall dwell
blessed for evermore, there henceforth abiding world
without end.   Amen.

PART II.—THE ASCENSION.

Seek thou earnestly, O illustrious man, that thou 440
mayst truly understand by the wisdom of thy soul,
deep searchings of spirit, how it came to pass that
the angels did not appear in robes of white when the
Almighty was born in pure nativity, what time the
Hero, the Prince, came to Bethlehem, having chosen
the sanctuary of Mary, flower of maidens, the virgin 445
renowned. Heralds were at hand who spake unto
the shepherds and proclaimed in words the true joy— 450
that the Son of God was born into the world in
Bethlehem. Yet it saith not in Scripture that at
that great tide they appeared in robes of white,
as they afterwards did when the glorious Prince, 455
the Lord triumphant, summoned to Bethany His
band of disciples, that company beloved. On that
joyful day they despised not the words of their
Master, the Bestower of goodly gifts. Soon were 460
they ready, the heroes with their Lord, [to go] unto
the holy city, where the Dispenser of glory, the
King of heaven, revealed many signs unto them in
parables, before the only-begotten Son, co-eternal 465

17

with His own Father, ascended on high, forty days
after He arose from the dust of death. Thus through
His passion had He fulfilled the words of the prophets
470 as of old they had sung throughout the world. The
disciples magnified Him, and gratefully adored the
Lord of life, the Father of all created things. Wherefore to His beloved comrades gave He a noble
reward, and these words spake the Prince of angels,
475 the mighty Ruler, as He was about to depart to His
Father's kingdom : 'Rejoice in spirit; never will
I forsake you, but will for aye continue my love
toward you, granting you strength, and abiding with
you for ever and ever, so that through my grace
480 ye shall know the lack of no good thing. Go forth
now over all the spacious earth, far-reaching ways;
declare unto the multitudes, preach and proclaim
the bright faith ; baptize the peoples beneath the
485 welkin, turning them to the skies; destroy the
shrines of idols, overthrow them, abhor them; blot
out enmity, and in the fulness of power sow peace
within men's souls. Henceforth I will abide with
you for your comfort, and will everywhere keep you
490 in peace, in strength unfailing.'

Then on a sudden loud music was heard in the
sky; a throng of heavenly angels, a radiant host,
messengers from glory, in legion came. Our King

departed through the temple's roof while they 495
looked on — those chosen retainers who were still
watching in that place of conference the footprints
of their beloved Lord. They saw their Master, the
Son of God, ascend from earth to heaven. Sad
were their souls, hot their sorrowing hearts within 500
their breasts, since now no longer might they behold
beneath heaven the One so dear. The heavenly
messengers raised a song; they praised the Lord,
magnified the Author of life, rejoicing in the
light that shone from the Savior's head. Then saw 505
they two glistening angels, fair shining in their
splendor round that first-born Son, the Glory of
kings. From on high they called with wondrous
words, with ringing speech, over the multitude of
men : 'Ye men of Galilee, why wait ye thus about ? 510
Ye plainly see the righteous King, the Lord of
victory, ascending unto heaven ; the First of princes,
the Creator of all peoples, will go up hence with 515
this angel-band to His dwelling-place, the Father's
royal seat. With such a throng, with this joyful host,
shall we bear the Lord — the noblest and best of all 520
the sons of glory — far up through heaven's vault
unto that beautiful city, Him[1] whom ye now gaze

[1] Possibly *đe* may go back to *gedryht* for its antecedent. Cf. the
parallel expression in line 570.

upon and with joy behold shining in splendor; yet shall He once again visit the nations of earth
525 with a host innumerable, and then shall He judge every deed performed by mortals beneath the skies.'

Then was the Lord of glory, King of archangels, Protector of saints, encompassed with clouds far above the dwellings [of men]. Joy and gladness
530 were renewed throughout the [celestial] habitations at the coming of the Prince. The eternal Source of joy sat down at the right hand of the Father, rejoicing in His victory.

To Jerusalem, the holy city, went the valiant
535 heroes sad of heart from the place where with their eyes they had but now beheld their God ascending, the Giver of joy. A fountain of tears [1] gushed forth; their constant love was overwhelmed with sorrow, hot within their breasts; their hearts
540 were stirred, their souls burned within them. For full ten days the illustrious disciples awaited in that bright city the promises of the Lord, as Himself commanded, the King of heaven, the Ruler of all, ere
545 He ascended into the far recesses of the skies.

---

1 *Wōpes hring* — a difficult phrase to translate. It occurs also *An.* 1280; *El.* 1132; *Gu.* 1313. Professor Cook, referring to Shelley, *Adonais* XI. 4–5; Browning, *By the Fireside* 149–150, suggests as a possible interpretation 'a circling fountain of tears,' tear-drops being likened to pearls upon a string, or beads in a necklace or rosary.

Shining angels came to meet the Giver of bliss to men. True it is, as the Scripture relates, that at that holy tide angels resplendent descending from the sky came unto Him in legions. Then arose great rejoic- 550 ing in heaven. It was indeed fitting that liegemen, a radiant host, brightly clad, should come unto that feast in the city of the Lord ; welcome was He whom they saw [sitting] on His throne, the King 555 of heaven, Giver of life to men, ruling in splendor the whole earth and the angelic host.

'Now[1] hath the Holy One despoiled hell of all the tribute which of old it wrongfully swallowed up into 560 that place of strife. Vanquished now are the devils' warriors, brought low and bound in living torments, bereft of glory in the abyss of hell. His adversaries[2] could not prevail in battle, in the hurling of weapons, 565 what time the King of glory, Guardian of heaven's realm, waged war against His ancient foes by His sole might, when He led forth from bondage, from the city of fiends, the greatest of spoils, a countless multitude of people, even the host which ye here 570 gaze upon. And now after the conflict the Savior

[1] Professor Cook interprets this speech as a continuation of that which ends at line 526. At first it is the disciples who are addressed; at line 575 it is the ascending host.

[2] Reading *wiðerbreocan* with Cosijn.

of souls, God's own Son, is minded to seek the throne
of spiritual grace.   Thus ye may understand who is
575 the Lord that leadeth this host. — Now go ye forth
boldly to meet your friends, joyful in spirit.   Open,
ye gates ;[1] through you the King, the Ruler of all, the
Author of creation, will lead into the city, unto the
580 joy of joys, the mighty host which He hath wrested
from the demons by His victory.   There shall be
fellowship between angels and men from this time
forth and for evermore.   There is now a covenant
between God and man, a sacred pledge — love, hope
585 of life, and joy in perfect light.'

Lo ! we have heard how the   st-child by
His advent brought again salvation ;   He, the
Creator's noble Son, freed and kept me   beneath
the clouds, so that now each mortal, while he dwell-
590 eth here in life, may choose either the shame of
hell or the fame of heaven, the shining day or the
loathsome night, the power of glory or the pain of
darkness, joy with the Lord or wailing with demons,
595 bliss [2] with angels or torment with fiends, either
life or death, whichsoever he preferreth to achieve
while body and soul abide in the world.   Where-

[1] From Ps. 24. 7.
[2] Lit. 'glory.'

fore let blessing and eternal thanks be unto the glory of the Trinity !

It is meet and right that all nations should give 600 thanks unto the Lord for every blessing which now and aforetime He hath ever bestowed upon us through the mystery of wonders manifold. · He giveth us food and abundance of riches, wealth throughout the broad earth, and fair weather 605 beneath the shelter of the sky. The sun and moon, brightest of stars, heaven's candles, shine for all men on the earth. Dew and rain descend; they call forth plenty for the nourishment of man, 610 and increase the riches of earth. For all this, therefore, we ought to give thanks and praise unto our Lord, but especially for the salvation granted for our joy, when by His ascension He 615 brought to end the misery we had so long endured, when the only-begotten King settled for mankind that greatest of feuds with His beloved[1] Father. For our soul's peace He abolished the sentence which had been pronounced in anger to the woe of man : 'I 620 created thee of earth;[2] upon it shalt thou dwell in misery, living in strife and suffering torment, chanting the death-song to thy foe's delight; and to

[1] Or, 'own.'
[2] From Gen. 3. 19.

the same shalt thou turn again, teeming with
625 worms; thence from the earth shalt thou afterwards
seek the fire of punishment.' Lo! this [curse]
did the Lord abate for us when He took on Him
the seed of man, body and limbs. When the Son
of the Creator, the God of hosts, was about to
630 ascend to the home of angels, at that holy tide
there arose [in Him] the desire to help us wretched
ones.

Concerning this Job fashioned a song, as he well
knew how; he praised the Protector of men, lauded
635 the Savior, and out of his love devised a surname
for the Son of God; He gave him the name of Bird,
which, by the power of the divine Spirit, the Jews
could not understand; the flight of that Bird was
640 secret and hidden from His enemies on earth, from
those who had a darkened mind and a stony heart
within their breasts; they would not recognize the
glorious miracles, many and various, which the noble
Son of God performed before them on the earth.
645 And thus the beloved Bird essayed flight: now
bold and strong in virtue He aspired the home
of angels, that fair abode; now through the Spirit's
grace He sought the precincts of earth and wended
650 His way to the world. Of Him the prophet sang:[1]

---

[1] Cf. Ps. 8. 1; 18. 10; 47. 5.

'He was lifted up, high and holy, in the arms of angels, in the fulness of His power, above the majesty of heaven.' They who made denial of the ascension could not perceive the flight of the Bird, 655 and believed not that the Author of life, the Holy One, in the likeness of man was lifted up from earth above the heavenly host. .

Then He who created the earth, God's Spirit-son, honored us and granted us gifts, eternal seats amid 660 the angels on high; moreover He sowed manifold wisdom, and planted it within the souls of men. Unto the mind [1] of one, through the Spirit of His mouth, 665 He sendeth wise eloquence and noble understanding; such an one can sing and speak many things; unto his soul is committed the power of wisdom. One can awaken the harp before warriors, touching it full loudly with his fingers. One can set forth 670 aright the law divine. One can tell the course of the stars, the expanse of [2] creation. One can skilfully write the spoken word. To one He giveth victory in war, when bowmen send the storm of darts, the winged arrows, over their shields. One can 675 boldly urge forward his bark over the salt sea, and stir the raging deep. One can climb the steep and

[1] Lit. 'memory of his mind.'
[2] Lit. 'wide.'

lofty tree. One can fashion the sword, the well-
680 tempered weapon. One knoweth the compass of
the plains, the far-reaching ways. So to us the
Ruler, the Son of God, doth dispense His gifts on
earth. But to no man will He give all wisdom of
soul, lest, exalted above others by his own power,
685 his pride work him evil.

Thus doth God almighty, King of creation, enrich
the progeny of earth with gifts and endowments
manifold; so also He bestoweth glory upon the
blessed of heaven; He establisheth peace for men
690 and angels unto all eternity.

So He honoreth His handiwork. Concerning this
the prophet said[1] that holy gems were lifted up on
high, the sun and moon, those radiant stars of
695 heaven. What indeed are those gems so bright
but God Himself? He is the Sun of righteousness, a glorious Light to angels and dwellers on
earth. The moon shineth over all the world, a
spiritual star; even so the Church of God shineth
700 brightly through the union of truth and righteousness — as the Scripture saith — since the Son
of God, King of all who are pure, arose from the
earth. Before that the church of the law-abiding
705 suffered persecution under the rule of heathen shep-

---

[1] Hab. 3. 11, according to the Septuagint.

herds. Then evil-doers recked not of the truth nor of their soul's need; but they rent and burned the temple of God, they overthrew and destroyed, they wrought deeds of blood. But after the ascension of the Lord eternal, triumph came to God's servants 710 through grace of the Spirit.

Of this sang Solomon, the son of David, ruler of nations, versed in the hidden things of song, and these words he spake:[1] 'This shall be made known, 715 that the Savior, the King of angels, strong in might, shall ascend the mountains, leaping the lofty downs; He shall encompass the mountains and hills with His glory, and by that noble leap He shall redeem the world and all the inhabitants of earth.'

The first leap was when He descended unto the 720 virgin, that spotless maid, and took on Him the likeness of man, yet without sin; that was for the comfort of all the dwellers on earth. The second leap was the birth of the infant, when the Glory of all glories, in the likeness of a child, lay in the manger 725 wrapped in [swaddling] clothes. The third leap, the bound of the King of heaven, was when He ascended the cross, the Father, the Spirit of comfort. The fourth leap was into the grave, when He came down from the tree, [and was held] fast in the

[1] Cant. 2. 8.

730 sepulchre. The fifth leap was when He cast the host of hell into living torment, and with fiery fetters bound their king within, that fierce spokes-735 man of fiends, where he lieth yet in prison, fastened with chains, bound by his sins. The sixth leap was the joyous revel of the Holy One, when He ascended to heaven, unto His former dwelling. At that holy time the angel-band grew merry with joy and glad-740 ness. They saw the King of glory, the Chief of princes, come unto His fatherland, unto the bright mansions. That exploit of the Prince was an eternal happiness to the blessed, the dwellers in the City.

Thus, while here on earth, the eternal Son of God 745 leaped boldly over the hills and lofty mountains. So must we mortals, in the thoughts of our hearts, leap from strength to strength and strive after glory, so that we may rise by our holy works to the high-750 est summit, where are hope and joy, a glorious band of liegemen. We have great need to follow after salvation with our hearts, to that place where we earnestly believe in our souls that the Saviour-son, the living God, hath ascended with 755 our human body.

Wherefore we should scorn all idle lusts, the wounds of sin, and rejoice in better things. We have for our comfort the Almighty, the Father in heaven. The Holy One on high will send His [760] angels hither to shield us against the deadly arrow-flights of evil-doers, lest the fiends inflict wounds upon us, when the author of evil sendeth forth the bitter arrow from his bended[1] bow among the people [765] of God. Wherefore we must ever be warily on our guard against the quick shot, lest the venomous point, the bitter dart, the sudden wile of fiends, penetrate beneath our flesh. Its hurt is grievous, [770] most livid of wounds. Let us then keep watch and ward while we abide here on earth! Let us beseech the Father for protection; let us pray the Son of God and the merciful Spirit that He who gave us life, body, limbs, and soul, will shield us against the [775] weapons of the foe, against the wiles of our enemies! Praise be to Him for ever, glory in the heavens world without end!

None of the race of men on earth need fear the shafts of devils, the spear-flights of the fierce ones, [780] if God, the Lord of hosts, protecteth him. The judgment is at hand when we shall obtain our reward, according as we have ever laid up for ourselves by our deeds on the broad earth. The [785] Scripture saith how in the beginning the Treasury of glory, God's noble Son, descended from on high,

---

[1] Perhaps this is the 'deceitful bow' of Ps. 78. 57; Hos. 7. 16.

and humbly came to earth into the virgin's womb.
790 Alas! I expect, yea, and fear a sterner doom when
the Prince of angels cometh again, since I have ill
kept those things which the Savior bade me in the
Scriptures. For this, as I account truth, I shall
behold terror, the punishment of sin, when many
795 shall be led into the assembly before the presence
of the eternal Judge.

　　Then shall the COURAGEOUS [1] tremble; he shall
hear the King, the Ruler of heaven, speak stern
words unto those who in time past ill obeyed Him
on earth, while as yet they could easily find comfort
800 for their YEARNING and their NEED. There in that
place shall many a one, weary and sore afraid,
await what dire punishment He will mete out to
them for their deeds. Gone is the WINSOMENESS
805 of earth's adornments. Long ago the portion of life's
joys granted Us was compassed about by LAKE-
FLOODS, our FORTUNE on the earth. Then shall our
treasures burn in fire; bright and swift shall the

---

　[1] The large type denotes the runes of the original which in succession spell the name of Cynewulf (in this poem, Cynwulf). These renderings (following Gollancz in the main) are partly conjectural; exactness, where that was possible, has been sacrificed in favor of the proper initials. It would be more correct to substitute *bold* for *courageous*, *misery* for *yearning*, *joy* for *winsomeness*, *sea* for *lakefloods*, *wealth* for *fortune*. Cosijn regards the letters, C., Y., and N. as forming *cyn* = 'mankind.'

red flame rage; fiercely shall it rush through the wide world. Plains shall perish, citadels fall. The fire shall be all astir; pitilessly shall that greediest of spirits waste the ancient treasure which men held of old, whilst pride abode with them upon the earth.

Wherefore I would exhort each beloved one that he neglect not his soul's need, nor be dissolved in vainglory, while God wills that he dwell here in the world, and that the soul journey in the tabernacle of the body. Every man should bethink him well in the days of his life that, according to the angel's word, the Lord of might first came to us benignly. He will be austere when He cometh again, stern and just. At that day the heavens shall shake and the mighty ends of the earth shall tremble; the bright King shall requite them for living on earth in evil deeds, guilty of sin. Wherefore weary in soul they shall long suffer fierce retribution in that bath of fire, hemmed in by surging [flames].

When the King of hosts shall come to the assembly with an innumerable throng, a widespread terror, the outcry of the lamenting, shall be loudly heard amid the sounds from heaven; the sorrowful, trusting but little in their works, shall wail before the face of the everlasting Judge. Then shall

arise a terror greater than was ever heard of on
840 earth from the beginning.   In that sudden hour
it shall be far dearer than all this fleeting world
unto every worker of iniquity to hide himself among
the victorious band, when the Lord of hosts, Chief
845 of princes, shall adjudge to all peoples, both friends
and foes, their just reward.   O great our need that
in this barren time, ere that horror, we earnestly
bethink us of the beauty of our souls!

850   Now is it as though we fared in ships out upon
the ocean, over the waters cold, and urged[1] our
barks, our sea-steeds, across the broad flood.   A
perilous stream it is, endless waves and wind-swept
855 seas, on which we toss throughout this fleeting world,
over the fathomless reaches.   Hard was our life
ere we sailed to land over the stormy main.   Then
860 came our help: God's Spirit-son guided us to the
haven of safety, and gave us grace to see, over
the vessel's side, where with firm-set anchor[2] we
should moor our sea-steeds, those ocean-stallions old.
·O let us fix our hope in that holy haven above,
865 which the Lord celestial prepared for us when He
ascended into the heavens!

[1] Lit. 'journeyed on.'
[2] Lit. 'fast at their anchors.'

PART III. — DOOMSDAY.

Lo ! at midnight, unawares, the great day of the Lord omnipotent shall mightily overtake the dwellers on earth, the bright creation ; as oft a daring robber, 870 a crafty thief, prowling about in darkness, in the murky night, suddenly comes upon careless men bound in sleep, and sorely assails them unprepared.

Then together unto Mount Zion shall ascend a 875 great multitude, radiant and joyful, the faithful of the Lord ; glory shall be theirs. Thereupon from the four corners of the world, from the uttermost regions of earth, angels all-shining shall with one 880 accord blow their crashing trumpets ; the earth shall tremble under men. Glorious and steadfast they shall sound together over against the course of the stars, chanting in harmony and making melody from south and from north, from east and from west, throughout the whole creation ; all man- 885 kind shall they wake from the dead unto the last judgment ; they shall rouse the sons of men all aghast from the ancient earth, bidding them straightway arise from their deep sleep.

33

There one may hear a sorrowing people, sad of
890 heart and greatly disquieted, sorely afraid and pitifully bewailing the deeds done in the body. This
shall be the greatest forewarning ever shown unto
men before or since. There all the hosts of angels
895 and of devils shall mingle, the fair and the swart;
there shall be a coming of both the white and the
black, according as an abode is prepared all unlike
for saints and sinners.

Then suddenly upon Mount Zion a blaze of the
900 sun, shining clear from the southeast, shall come
forth from the Creator, gleaming more brightly than
the mind of man can conceive, when the Son of God
shall appear hither through the vault of heaven.
All glorious from the eastern skies shall come the
905 presence of Christ, the aspect of the noble King,
gentle in spirit toward His own, bitter toward the
wicked, wondrously varied, diverse to the blessed
910 and the forlorn. Unto the good, the host of the
holy, He shall be joyful of countenance, radiant,
winsome, loving, gracious, and fair.[1] Sweet and
pleasant shall it be for His loved ones, for those
who in days of old pleased Him well by their words
and deeds, to gaze upon that shining face, winningly
915 benign, upon the advent of the King, the Lord of

---

[1] Lit. 'fair in joys.'

might. But unto the evil and wicked, unto those who shall come to Him undone by sin, He shall be terrible and awful to behold.

That[1] may be a prophetic[2] intimation to him who is wise of thought, that he shall have no cause whatever to be afraid; he shall not be dismayed in soul at the terror of the Presence, when he beholdeth the Lord of all creation approaching with mighty wonders to the doom of many, while on all sides press round Him a band of angels, a shining host, legions of the saints in great multitudes.

The vast creation shall resound, and the fiercest of raging fires shall sweep over the whole earth before the Lord; the fiery flame shall hurtle; the heavens shall burst asunder; all the firm-set flashing stars shall fall. The sun itself, which shone so brightly above the former world for the sons of men, shall be turned dark, even to the hue of blood; the moon, also, which of old gave light for mortals in the night season, shall fall headlong; and the stars shall be hurled from heaven by the fury of the storm-vexed air.

---

[1] The meaning of this passage is somewhat doubtful.

[2] The usual sense of *wites* is here inappropriate. I have accepted Professor Cook's suggestion (cf. his note on line 182) that in *wites* we may possibly have a form of the root *wit-*, as seen in *witga*, 'prophet.'

Now shall the Almighty, the glorious Prince,
Creator. of great kings, come into the assembly with
His angel band.   An exultant host of His retainers
shall be there also.   The souls of the blest shall
945 journey with their Lord, when the Protector of men
shall visit the nations of earth with dread punishment.   Then throughout the broad earth shall be
heard the piercing blast of the heavenly trump;
from seven quarters the winds shall rush, blowing
950 and roaring with awful crash, rousing and blighting
the world with storm, filling with terror[1] the whole
creation.   There shall be heard[2] a deafening uproar,
loud and violent, heavy and appalling, terrible unto
955 mortals, of all tumults the mightiest.

Then the cursed hosts of men shall turn in
throngs unto the all-embracing flame, and living
meet the deadly blaze, some above and some
beneath, filled with fire.   Certain is it that there
960 the race of Adam shall lament, a joyless people,
full of sorrows, afflicted by no trifling woes but by
the greatest of miseries, what time the livid surging
965 of fire, the dusky flame, shall seize far and wide on
all three àt once — ocean with its fish, earth with its
mountains, and highest heaven bright with its stars.

[1] Reading *fēre* with Cook.   Cf. his note on line 952.
[2] Lit. 'made manifest.'

Fiercely and cruelly shall the destroying flame burn all three together. At that dread time the whole earth shall mourn, and be sorely troubled.

Thus shall the all-devouring spirit, the ravaging fire, overrun the earth and its lofty structures; the [1] hot and greedy blast, famed afar, shall, over the earth's plain, fill the whole world with the terror of fire. The city-walls shall fall in ruins. Mountains shall melt away, along with the headlands which erstwhile firm and steadfast stoutly shielded the earth from ocean-floods, bulwarks against the waves and heaving waters. Then shall the death-fire seize on every creature, both bird and beast; the murky flame, a raging warrior, shall stride over the earth. Wheresoever the waters once flowed, the hurrying floods, there the fishes of the deep, cut off from ocean, shall be consumed in a bath of fire; every sea-monster exhausted shall die; water shall burn like wax. There shall be more wonders than mind of man can conceive — how whirlwind, and tempest, and raging blast shall rend the broad creation. Men shall wail; they shall weep and lament with mournful voices, downcast and wretched, overwhelmed with sorrow. The swart flame shall blaze on those fordone by sin; the fire shall consume the golden ornaments,

---

[1] The rendering of lines 973–4 is somewhat doubtful.

all the ancient treasure of the kings of the nations. There amid the sounds from heaven an outcry shall be [heard], wailing and lamentation, the strife of the living, loud weeping, and the sad plaint of men. 1000 Herefrom no man guilty of crime can win refuge, or anywhere escape from the flame, but that fire shall seize on all things throughout the earth; it shall fiercely delve and eagerly explore the regions of the 1005 world within and without, until the glowing flame hath wholly purged away by its billowing the stain of earthly sin.

Then in great majesty shall God almighty come to that dread mount; the holy King of heavenly angels, the Lord omnipotent, shall shine resplendent 1010 upon the multitudes; round about Him shall brightly gleam a most goodly throng, holy bands, the blessed company of angels; with terror of the Father shall they tremble, dismayed in their inmost thoughts. 1015 Wherefore it is no marvel that the unclean race of men should greatly fear and pitifully lament, since even the holy race, the white host of archangels, heaven-bright, are sore affrighted before that Presence, what time the radiant beings await with trembling 1020 the judgment of the Lord. Most terrible of all days shall that be in the world when the King of glory shall chasten all peoples by His might, and bid

speech-uttering men, tribe after tribe, arise from 1025
their graves and come every one unto the assembly.

Then shall the race of Adam assume flesh; there
shall be an end to their rest and sojourn in the earth.
At[1] Christ's coming every one of them shall arise in 1030
newness of life, shall take on body and limbs, and
again be made young; he shall have within him all
the good or evil which in former days on the earth,
in the circuit of years, he hath treasured within his
heart. He shall have together both body and soul. 1035
The aspect of his works, the memory of his words,
and the counsel of his heart, shall come to light
before the King of heaven.

Then shall the race of men be increased and renewed by the Creator; a great multitude shall ascend 1040
unto the judgment when the Author of life shall loose
the bonds of death. The air shall be enkindled;
the stars of heaven shall fall; the greedy flame shall
ravage far and wide. Spirits shall depart unto their
eternal abode. The deeds of mortals shall be 1045
brought to light throughout the world; in no wise
can men conceal their treasures, the thoughts of their
hearts, before that Prince; deeds shall not be hidden
from Him, but on that great day the Lord shall 1050
know in what sort every man hath merited eternal

---

[1] Lit. 'before.'

life, and all shall be revealed that they have
wrought in the world early or late. Naught of
man's thoughts shall be concealed, but that dread
1055 day shall bring to light all the secrets of his breast,
all the meditations of his heart. He must bethink
him aforetime of his spirit's need, who would bring
to God a radiant countenance when the hot con-
suming fire maketh trial before the victorious Judge
1060 how souls have been kept from sin.

Now the trumpet's blast, the bright ensign, and the
hot fire, the exalted host, the company of angels, the
pang of terror, the stern day, and the high rood
1065 raised aloft as a sign of sovereignty, shall summon
forward the multitude of men, the souls of all who
early or late have taken upon them body and limbs.
Then that mighty host, immortal and restored to
1070 youth, shall, eager or compelled, as they are called
by their names, pass into the presence of the Lord,
and bear before God's Son the secrets of their
hearts, the treasures of their souls. The Father
will perceive whether His sons bring untainted souls
1075 from the land in which they dwelt. They shall be of
good courage who bring unto the Creator a radiant
countenance; their might and joy, the glorious
reward of their works, shall be exceeding plenteous
as a recompense to their souls. Well is it for

them who at that dread time shall be acceptable 1080 unto God.

There shall sinful men, sad at heart, behold the greatest affliction. Not for their behoof shall the cross of our Lord, brightest of beacons, stand 1085 before all nations, wet with the pure blood of heaven's King, stained with His gore, shining brightly over the vast creation. Shadows shall be put to flight when the resplendent cross shall blaze upon all peoples. But this shall be [1] for an affliction 1090 and a punishment to men, to those malefactors who knew no gratitude to God, that He, the King, was crucified on the holy rood for the sins of mankind, on that day when He whose body knew no sin 1095 nor base iniquity lovingly purchased life for men with the price with which He ransomed us.[2] For all this will He rigorously exact [3] recompense when 1100 the red rood shall shine brightly over all in the sun's stead.

Fearfully and sorrowfully shall they look thereon, those black workers of iniquity, fordone by sin; they shall behold to their bale that which would 1105

---

[1] I have not translated the *geteod* of line 1090; it is inserted by Grein and later editors solely for metrical reasons.

[2] This passage may be corrupt. Cf. Cook's *Christ*, note on line 1097.

[3] Reading *gemonian* with Grein.

have been their greatest weal, had they been willing
to apprehend it as their good. With sad hearts
shall they behold the ancient gashes and open wounds
upon their Lord, where His foes pierced with nails
1110 the white hands and the holy feet, and let forth gore
from His side ; blood and water gushed forth together
before the eyes of all the people, when He was on
1115 the cross. All this they themselves shall then be
able to see, open and manifest, how He suffered
many things for the love of sinners. The sons of
men shall clearly behold how the false-hearted
1120 denied Him, mocked Him with blasphemies, spat
their spittle in His face, and spake insults against
Him ; how hell-doomed men, blind of thought, fool-
ish and erring, struck that blessed countenance with
their hands, with their outstretched palms, with
1125 their very fists, and round His head entwined a
cruel crown of thorns.

They saw that the dumb creation — verdant earth
and high heaven — shudderingly felt the sufferings
1130 of their Lord ; and though they had not life, yet
moaned in sorrow when wicked men seized on
their Savior with impious hands. The sun became
darkened, obscured by misery. In Jerusalem the
people saw how [1] that choicest of tapestries, which

[1] Reading *hū* with Grein.

the throng had been wont to look upon as the
glory of the holy house, was torn asunder from 1135
the top, so that it lay on the ground in two pieces;
the veil of the temple, wrought of wondrous colors
for the adornment of that house, was rent of itself in
twain, as if a sharp-edged sword had passed through 1140
it. Divers walls and stones throughout the world
burst wide asunder; the earth, stirred by terror,
quaked with a great noise; the broad sea showed
forth the power of its might, and fiercely broke 1145
from its confines over earth's bosom; and the stars
in their beauteous station forsook their aspect
sweet. At that same time heaven clearly recog-
nized who had nobly made it bright with starry 1150
gems on high; of a truth it sent its herald
when first was born the radiant King of creation. Lo! on that same day on which He suffered, even sinful men saw in sooth a wondrous
miracle — that the earth gave up those who lay 1155
within her; they rose up living, those, the dead
and buried, whom she had firmly confined, even
they who had kept in their hearts the Lord's command. Hell, the sin-avenging, also perceived that
the Creator, the sovereign Lord, was come, when it 1160
gave forth that host from its hot bosom; the
hearts of many were comforted, and sorrows van-

ished from their souls.   Lo ! even the sea declared
who had set it on its broad bed, the almighty King,
1165 for it made itself passable unto Him when God
willed to go over its waves ; the water-flood durst
not flow with its billows over its Master's feet.
1170 Trees likewise many, and by no means few, declared
who had shaped them with their branches,[1] when
almighty God ascended one of them and suffered
pain for men's weal, loathsome death for the help
of mankind.   Then was many a tree suffused with
1175 bloody tears beneath its bark, red and frequent ; the
sap turned to gore.   The inhabitants of earth cannot
tell, with all their wisdom, how many things that
have no feeling, lifeless things, felt then the Lord's
1180 sufferings.   The noblest of the races of earth and
heaven's high creation — all became sad and dismayed for that[2] alone.   Although by their nature
they had no understanding, yet miraculously did
1185 they apprehend when their Lord departed the body.
Blind-hearted men, harder than flint, could not recognize the Savior, nor that the Lord, God almighty,
had saved them from hell-torment by His holy
1190 might.   From the beginning of the world far-seeing
men, prophets of God, holy and wise of heart,

[1] Perhaps 'fruits,' or 'blossoms.'
[2] Or 'them,' or 'Him.'

not once but oft through their wise understanding declared unto men this very thing concerning the glorious Son — that, through the noble maid, He, the Lord of glory, the Author of bliss, the Precious Stone, should become a refuge and comfort to all 1195 men in the world.

What can he expect who refuseth to keep in mind the Savior's gentle precepts, and all the afflic- 1200 tions that He endured for men because of His desire that we should possess the home of glory unto all eternity? On the dread day of that great judgment, sad shall it be for him who, defiled by 1205 deadly sins, must look upon the scars, the wounds, the sufferings of the Lord. With aching hearts shall they see the greatest of sorrows; them did the King Himself, through His merciful spirit, redeem 1210 from sin with His own body, that they might live without iniquity, and enjoy the eternal blessedness of glory; but they gave no thanks unto their Lord for this heritage, wherefore the unhappy ones shall see to their sorrow signs manifest in such as are 1215 good.

When Christ shall sit on His royal throne, on the high seat, then shall the Father almighty, the radiant Creator, God of the heavenly hosts, Ruler of the skies, adjudge righteously to each band 1220

according to their deeds. Then shall be gathered on His right hand the folk undefiled, chosen by the election of Christ Himself, those who in the days of their life have faithfully and joyfully obeyed His
1225 commandments; but to the Creator's left side shall be assigned the workers of iniquity: the righteous King of victory shall bid the sinful host depart unto His left hand. There, detected, they shall wail
1230 and tremble in terror before the Lord; an impure people, foul as goats, they can expect no mercy. Then in the presence. of God shall be determined for the generations of men the doom of their souls, according as they have wrought erewhile.

Three signs shall there be visible together unto
1235 the blessed, inasmuch as they have well kept their Lord's will in word and deed.

First shall appear this — that they shall shine with light before the nations, with glory and splendor over the habitations of cities; their former deeds shall
1240 shine upon each one of them brighter than the sun.

The second shall likewise be manifest — that they shall know their Sovereign's grace in the bestowal of [1] glory, and shall see, to their eyes' delight, that
1245 they may possess bright joys in the heavenly kingdom, blessed amid the angels.

[1] Cf. Cook's *Christ*, note on line 1243.

The third shall be that the happy band shall behold the lost, that host of burning creatures, suffering pain in the misery of darkness, as a punishment for their sins — raging fire and the bite of 1250 serpents with bitter jaws; from this shall spring up a winsome joy for them. When they shall see others suffer the evil that they escaped through the Savior's mercy, they shall the more earnestly 1255 thank God for the bliss and happiness which they behold — that He hath both saved them from perdition and granted them eternal joys ; hell shall be locked against them, the kingdom of heaven shall be granted unto them. This shall be given as reward to those that ever faithfully kept the Crea- 1260 tor's will in love.

Far different shall be the joy of the others ; they can see in themselves too many woes — countless sins, iniquities aforetime committed. Tribulation 1265 and dire evil shall cleave unto the sorrowing ones in three ways.

One is that they shall see before them too many miseries, dread hell-fire, prepared for their punishment, in which, suffering torment, they shall for 1270 aye endure damnation.

There shall also be a second misery for the shame of the sinful — that the lost shall suf-

fer there the greatest disgrace; the Lord shall see
1275 in them loathsome sins by no means few; so, too,
the shining band of heavenly angels, the sons of
men, all the dwellers on earth, and the fell fiend,
shall behold the power of darkness, all the iniqui-
1280 ties. Through the body they may see the grievous
sins in their souls; their sinful flesh shall be shamefully transpierced, as if it were clear glass, through
which one may most easily look.

The third shall be a sorrow and sore grief for
1285 the wretched — that they behold how the joyful, the
righteous, rejoice in the good deeds which they, the
unhappy ones, scorned to do while days were still
theirs; and concerning their own works it shall be
1290 a grievous tribulation that they had freely wrought
unrighteousness. They shall see the better ones
shine in glory; their own misery shall not be their
sole punishment, but the happiness of others shall be
to them a grief, because in former days they forsook
1295 joys so fair and sweet for the delusive pleasure of
the body, the vain lust of the sinful flesh. There,
ashamed and distressed by their ignominy, they
shall wander dizzily about; they shall bear their
evil works, the burden of their sin; on that shall
1300 the people gaze.

Wherefore it had been better for them had they

felt shame before one man for every evil deed and transgression, had they told God's messenger that they knew to their sorrow the sins within them. The confessor cannot look through the flesh into 1305 the soul [to discover] whether a man speaketh truth or falsehood concerning himself, when he confesseth[1] his sins. One can, however, heal every transgression, every unclean sin, if he but tell it to one. man ; but none on that dread day can con- 1310 ceal the crime unatoned ; multitudes shall there behold it.

O that we might now see with the eyes of our body the deadly iniquities in our souls, the wounds of sin, the wicked thoughts, the impure imaginings ! 1315

No[2] one can tell another with what eagerness each should[3] strive in every way to sustain his life and anxiously prolong his existence, wash away the rust of sin and chasten himself, and remove the 1320 defilement of a former wound during the brief span of life here below; so that before the eyes of the dwellers on earth he may enjoy an abode among men, blameless and unashamed, while body and 1325 soul may yet dwell together.

[1] The usual translation of *bigān* is ' to commit.'

[2] This paragraph seems out of keeping with the context; cf. Cook's *Christ*, note on line 1316.

[3] Lit. ' will.'

Now must we look sharply and earnestly with the eyes of the heart through the soul's covering upon the sin beneath. With our other eyes, the jewels 1330 of the head, we can in no way look through the seat[1] of thought [to see] whether good or evil dwelleth within each one, so that at that dread time he may be acceptable unto God.

When from His lofty throne the high King of 1335 heaven shall shine in glory, with a dazzling light, over every nation, then shall He first speak unto the blessed, before the angels and before all nations, and graciously promise them love ; He shall gently 1340 comfort them with His holy speech, and shall proclaim peace to them ; He shall bid them depart safe and sanctified to the land of angels' bliss, and joyfully possess it world without end :

'Receive ye now with friends my Father's kingdom, the bliss and the glory and the fair beauty 1345 of that home which was joyfully prepared for you before all ages, against the time when with the best beloved ye might behold the riches of life eternal, the precious joys of heaven. This indeed ye mer- 1350 ited when with compassionate hearts ye willingly received the poor and needy. When in my name they humbly besought mercy of you, then did ye help

[1] Lit. 'soul.'

them and give them shelter, bread to the hungry and clothing to the naked; those that lay sick in pain, 1355 grievously suffering, bound by disease, ye gently strengthened in spirit with the affection of your hearts. For me ye did all this when ye sought them in love, and with consolation stayed their spirits. For this shall ye long enjoy a fair reward 1360 with my loved ones.'

Then with far different words, with fearful menace, shall God almighty begin to address the evil ones on His left hand. They need not then 1365 expect mercy from the Lord, neither life nor grace, but recompense for their words and deeds shall fall to men, to those endowed with speech, according to their works; they shall suffer the one righteous doom, full of terror. On that day the 1370 great compassion of the Almighty shall be withdrawn from the dwellers on earth, when with bitter words He fiercely chargeth their sins upon the stubborn-hearted, and commandeth them to render account of the lives which He had given the sinful 1375 for their weal. Then shall the Lord almighty begin to speak as if to one alone, and yet shall He mean the whole band of the sinful:

'Lo! I wrought thee, O man, of old with my hands, and gave thee understanding; I formed for 1380

thee limbs of clay and gave thee a living spirit;
I honored thee above all creatures, and caused
thee to have form and aspect like unto myself;
I gave thee fulness of power and wealth over
all spacious lands; thou knewest naught of the
1385 woe and darkness that thou wast to suffer. Yet
for this thou wast not grateful. When I had
shaped thee so beautiful and winsome, and had
given thee power that thou mightst rule over the
creatures of earth, I set thee in the fair region
1390 to enjoy the rich luxuriance and bright hues of
Paradise;[1] thou wouldst not obey the word of life,
but at the bidding of thy destroyer didst break
my commandment; thou didst rather hearken to
1395 the wily foe, the perfidious fiend, than to thy
Creator. Now will I pass over that ancient tale,
how thou didst first devise evil and didst lose by
thy wicked deeds what I had granted thee for thy
weal. When I had bestowed upon thee so many
1400 blessings, and when to thy mind it seemed too little
happiness unless thou mightst have fulness of
power equal to God's, then to thy foes' delight didst
thou become estranged from that joy, cast out afar;
sad of heart, cheerless and sinful, deprived of all
1405 blessings and joys, thou wast forced to give up

---

[1] Somewhat freely rendered.

the glory of Paradise, the abode of spirits; thou
wast driven into the dark world, where long thereafter thou didst suffer great hardships, sorrow and 1410
grievous toil, and swart death, and after thy depar-
ture, bereft of helpers, wast doomed to fall headlong
down to hell.

'Then it began to repent me that my handiwork
should fall into the power of fiends, that the off- 1415
spring of man should see destruction, should learn
to know an inhospitable abode and sore vicissitudes.
Thereupon I myself descended as a child into my
mother, yet her virginity was wholly inviolate. I 1420
was the Only-begotten for the help of men. With
their hands they swathed me, wrapped me in the gar-
ments of the poor, and laid me in darkness, wound
about with sable raiment. Lo! this I endured for
the world! Little did I seem unto the sons of men;
on the hard stone I lay, a young child in the 1425
manger, in order that I might put away from thee the
torment and hot misery of hell; that thou mightst
shine holy and blessed in life eternal, for that I
suffered the pain.

'It was not out of pride, but in my youth I
endured suffering and shameful pain of body that
through it I might become like unto thee, and that 1430
thou, freed from sin, mightst become like me in

aspect; because of my love for man, my head bore
the grievous blow. Nor was my face spared :[1] often
1435 my countenance received spittle from the mouths
of the impious, the workers of iniquity. They
cruelly mixed for me a sour drink of vinegar and
gall. For mankind's sake I endured the hatred
1440 of foes; they pursued me with outrages — they
shrank not from deadly hostility — and smote me
with scourges. All that pain, scorn, and abuse, I
humbly bore for thee. About my head they wound
1445 a sharp and cruel crown, and pitilessly pressed it
on; of thorns was it wrought. Then was I hanged
upon a lofty tree, fastened to a cross. And straightway with a spear they let forth from my side blood
and gore upon the earth, that through it thou
1450 mightst be saved from the devil's tyranny. Sinless,
I suffered punishment and sore torment, until I gave
up from my body the living ghost. Behold now
the deadly wounds which they made in my hands
1455 and feet, by which I hung there, cruelly fastened;
here canst thou also see, still visible, the bloody
wound in my side.

'How unequal was the reckoning betwixt us
1460 two! I bore thy pain that thou, happy and blessed,
mightst possess my kingdom; and by my death I

---

[1] Lit. 'My face suffered.'

dearly bought long life for thee, that thenceforth
thou mightst dwell in light, radiant and free from
sin.   My body, which had harmed no man, lay 1465
buried in the earth, hidden beneath in the tomb,
that thou mightst dwell in splendor in the skies
above, mighty amid the angels.

'Why didst thou forsake that glorious life which
out of love I graciously bought for thee with my 1470
body, as a help to the wretched?   Thou wast so
witless that thou didst not render thanks unto the
Lord for thy redemption.   Naught demand I now
for that bitter death which I suffered for thee; but 1475
do thou give unto me thy life, for which, in martyr-
dom, I once gave up mine own as ransom; I claim
that life which thou to thine own disgrace hast sin-
fully destroyed by thy transgressions.   Why didst
thou, through evil lusts and foul sin, wilfully defile
that tabernacle which I consecrated in thee as my 1480
sweet[1] home of joy?   Yea, working iniquity, thou
didst shamefully pollute the body which I redeemed
for myself from the power of fiends, and then for- 1485
bade it sin.   Why hast thou crucified me on the
cross of thy hands more painfully than when I hung
of old?   O, this one, methinks, is more grievous!
Now is the cross of thy sins, on which I am bound 1490

[1] Or, 'own.'

unwillingly, more bitter to me than was that other
which I ascended of my own free will, what time thy
misery grieved my heart most sorely, when I drew
thee forth from hell — if only thou hadst been willing to hold to it henceforth !

1495　'I in this world was poor, that thou mightst be
rich in heaven; I was wretched in thy homeland,
that thou in mine mightst be blessed.　Yet for all
this thou wast in no wise grateful in soul unto thy
Savior.

'I commanded you that ye should cherish well
1500 my brethren in this earthly kingdom, and help the
needy with those possessions which I gave to you on
earth.　Ill have ye performed it; ye have forbidden
the poor to enter beneath your roof, and with hard
1505 hearts have denied them everything — raiment to
the naked, food to the hungry.　Though, weary and
feeble, distressed for drink, void of all sustenance
and parched with thirst, they prayed for water in my
name, ye did insolently deny them.　Ye sought not
1510 out the sorrowful, nor spake to them a kindly word
of comfort, that they might pluck up a more buoy-
ant spirit within their breasts.　All this ye did in
scorn of me, the King of heaven.　Wherefore ye
shall endure sore punishment for ever, suffering
torment with demons.'

Then over them all, over the doomed folk, the [1515]
Lord of victories shall Himself send forth a dread
decree, full of tribulation — He shall say to the
host of sinful souls :

‘ Depart[1] now, accursed, by your own wills dis-
possessed of the angels’ joy, into everlasting fire, [1520]
hot and fierce, which was prepared for Satan and
his followers, for the devil and his black crew; into
that shall ye fall headlong.’   Nor can they, bereft
of resource, disregard the command of heaven’s [1525]
King; those who erstwhile strove against God shall
straightway fall into that horrid abyss.   Then shall
the Lord of sovereign sway be stern and mighty,
terrible and full of wrath.   No foe upon this earth
can then abide His presence.

With His right hand shall He swing the victor- [1530]
sword so that the devils shall fall down into the
deep pit, the sinful band into the dusky flame, the
fated spirits beneath earth’s surface, the corrupt
and damned crew to perdition in the abode of
fiends, the house of torment, the death-hall of the [1535]
devil.   Thereafter they shall in no wise come to the
remembrance of the Lord; they shall not escape
from sin, but, guilty of crimes, wrapped in flame,
they shall there suffer death.   The punishment for

[1] With evident reference to Matt. 25. 41.

1540 transgression shall stand revealed before them; it is torment everlasting. Never can the burning abyss in that eternal night purge away the sin of the dwellers in hell, the stain of their souls; but the deep, bottomless pit shall feed the disconsolate, and 1545 hold the spirits in darkness; it shall burn them with its ancient flame and with its terrible frost; it shall afflict the multitudes with hateful serpents, with countless torments, with jaws deadly and terrible.

Of this may we be certain, with one voice may we 1550 speak and truly declare, that he hath lost his soul's keeper, the wisdom of life, who heedeth not now whether his spirit is to be sad or joyous in that place where after death it shall abide for ever. He 1555 feareth not, rash man, to commit sin, nor hath he aught of regret within his soul lest because of his misdeeds the Holy Spirit should depart from him in this fleeting time.

Then the sinner, black and guilty of death, cursed 1560 for his crimes, shall stand trembling before the Lord at the judgment; the transgressor, unworthy of eternal life, shall be filled with fire, and overwhelmed with terror in the presence of God; ghastly and hideous, he shall have the hue of the damned, the 1565 sign of a life of guilt. Then shall the sons of iniquity pour out their tears and bewail their sins, when the time is past; but too late shall they seek help for their souls, for[1] the Lord of hosts will not heed how the doers of evil sorely bewail their ancient treasures at that all-revealing time. That 1570 sorrowful season will not be granted to the peoples, in order that he who obtaineth not his life's redemption while dwelling here may there find salvation. There no grief shall be shown to the good, nor weal 1575 to the wicked; but each one shall bring before [God] his own work.

Therefore he who desireth to have life[2] with the Creator should bestir himself while body and spirit are joined together. Let him zealously foster the 1580 beauty of his soul according to God's will, and be careful in word and deed, in thought and conduct, while this world, speeding with its shadows, may still shine for him; so that he lose not in this 1585 fleeting time the blessedness of his joy and the fulness of his days, the beauty of his work and the reward of glory, which the righteous King of heaven shall give at that holy tide as a meed of victory to those who in spirit obey Him with gladness. 1590

Then shall heaven and hell be fulfilled with the sons of men, with the souls of mortals. The deeps shall swallow God's adversaries; tossing flame shall

---

[1] Lit. 'when.'   [2] Reading *líc* with Grein.

1595 harass wicked men, those arch-malefactors, and shall
not let them depart thence in joy to a place of
safety; but the fire shall hold the multitude fast,
and vex the sons of iniquity. Foolhardy methink-
eth it that beings endowed with souls should take
1600 no heed, when they commit[1] sin, what the Lord
hath prescribed as penalty for them, the people of
his foes. When life and death shall devour souls,
the house of torment shall stand open and revealed
1605 before the perjurers, and sinful men shall fill it with
their black souls. Then as a punishment for iniquity
the guilty host shall be cut off, the base from the
holy, unto terrible destruction. There thieves and
1610 robbers, the lying and adulterous, need not hope for
life, and the forsworn shall see retribution for sin,
severe and awful. Then shall hell receive the host
of the faithless, and the Lord shall give them over
to the fiends unto perdition; the damned shall
1615 suffer mortal agony most grievous. Wretched shall
he be who chooseth to deserve by his transgressions
that at the judgment day he shall be separated as a
guilty man from his Savior unto death below, among
1620 the hosts of hell, in the hot fire, beneath barriers of
flame; there shall they stretch forth their limbs to
be bound, and burned, and scourged, as a punishment

---

[1] Reading *fremmað* with Grein.

for sin. Then the Holy Ghost, through the power
of God, shall at the King's command lock up hell,
chiefest of all the houses of torment, filled with fire 1625
and the host of fiends. That is the greatest of
agonies for both devils and men. It is a joyless
abode. There none can ever escape from the cold
fetters. They broke the King's command, the sub-
lime precept of the Scriptures; wherefore those 1630
who here scorned the glory[1] of the heavenly realm
must dwell in eternal night, and, guilty of sin,
thenceforth endure their everlasting pain.

But the elect shall bring before Christ bright
treasures; their glory shall live at the judgment 1635
day; they shall possess the joy of a tranquil life with
God, such as is granted unto every saint in the kingdom of heaven. That is the home which shall have
no end, and there for evermore the sinless shall 1640
possess their joy, and, clothed with light, enfolded
in peace, shielded from sorrows, honored by joys,
endeared to the Savior, shall praise the Lord, the
beloved Protector of life; radiant with grace they
shall enjoy in bliss the fellowship of angels, and 1645
worship the Guardian of men for ever and ever.
The Father of all shall have and hold dominion over
the hosts of the sanctified.

[1] Or, perhaps, 'Lord.'

There is song of angels, joy of the blest; there
1650 is the dear presence of the Lord, brighter than
the sun unto the blessed; there is the love of
dear ones; life without death; a joyous multitude
of men; youth without age; the glory of the
heavenly hosts; health without pain; rest with-
1655 out toil for the workers of righteousness; bliss of
the happy; day without darkness, bright and glad-
some; happiness without sorrow; harmony without
strife 'twixt friends rejoicing in heaven; peace
without enmity in the congregation of the saints.
1660 No hunger shall be there, nor thirst, nor sleep, nor
sore disease, nor scorching of the sun, nor cold,
nor care; but there the company of the blest, most
radiant of hosts, shall for aye enjoy the grace of
their King and glory with their Lord.

Lightning Source UK Ltd.
Milton Keynes UK
23 February 2011

168066UK00005B/92/P

9 781147 312423